LIFE ON
THE FISHING
FLEET

ANTHONY BURTON

IMPORTANT DATES

1088   Yarmouth granted a charter as a Free Market for the fishing industry.

1357   The Statute of Herrings establishes the first government regulations of the sale of fish.

c.1380   'Gibbing', the process of preserving herring in salt, is invented in Zeeland in the Netherlands.

1412   English boats fish in Icelandic waters for the first time.

1532–41   Conflict between Holland and Scotland after Scots ban Dutch boats from their waters.

1786   Formation of British Fishery Society to promote the development of the industry, especially in Scotland.

1788   Britain's first steam-powered vessel is launched.

1790   Launch of the *Original*, the first purpose-built lifeboat.

1801   Thomas Telford appointed to begin a programme of improving old and building new fishing harbours in Scotland.

1809   The government authorises a bounty of £5 per ton on fish caught by whole-decked vessels.

1824   Royal National Lifeboat Institution is founded.

1848   Storm on the Scottish east coast: 124 boats are sunk and 100 lives lost.

1877   A paddle steamer is used as a trawler for the first time.

1881   The Eyemouth disaster: 189 lives are lost.

1910   A diesel engine is given its first trial in a British vessel and is soon adopted for use in fishing boats.

1958   Start of the First Cod War, as Iceland tries to impose a ban on British fishing round her coast.

1970   The European Union agrees to adopt a Common Fishing Policy to attempt to preserve fish stocks.

1976   Iceland and the UK reach agreement on fishing rights.

2013   The European Parliament agrees to begin a major review of the Common Fishing Policy.

INTRODUCTION

At the end of the 19th century, the British fishing industry was a huge concern at the very peak of its prosperity. In 1881 it was estimated that the country had 22,000 merchant vessels but 30,000 fishing boats. These were manned by 100,000 men and boys and another 100,000 worked onshore in related trades. When did this great industry begin?

No one can really say when the inhabitants of these islands first started catching fish for food, but we do know that it began long before the first written records appeared. When the amazingly well-preserved Neolithic site of Skara Brae on Orkney was excavated, archaeologists found large quantities of discarded fish bones, so although we know nothing of the methods they used we can at least be certain that the people living here some 4,500 years ago were catching and eating fish.

Moving closer to our own time, there is compelling evidence that the Vikings fished from small boats using lines and hooks, and there is equally good evidence that they brought the technology with them when they settled in parts of northern Britain. Early medieval fishing boats – open boats with one mast carrying a single square sail – were based on Scandinavian models.

Over the next few centuries the industry diversified. Each region developed its own style of boat construction suited to its own particular needs. Diverse techniques were used to catch different types of fish. Some were still caught on hooked lines; others were captured using different types of net and different techniques. One thing, however, remained constant: fishing has always been an occupation fraught with danger, and still is to this day.

◄ The simplest fishing boats were open with a single mast, like these Scottish vessels.

HOOK, LINE AND SINKER

Line fishing is one of the oldest methods of catching fish, dating back to prehistory, and it continues to this day. It can be carried out in small boats launched off a beach and working close to shore, or by larger vessels working far out to sea. The technology is simple: a line of baited hooks is thrown overboard with a heavy weight, the sinker, to carry it down to the seabed. It can be used for catching a wide variety of fish. In southern England, line fishing for mackerel has always been common, while further north in Scotland, cod and halibut were the main catch.

The cod fisheries of Scotland developed from the 16th century with a growing trade in salt cod. It was a way of life that occupied the whole population of many fishing villages. Small line fishing was carried out inshore. Women would be

out on the beach early in the morning collecting mussels, which were used for bait, and they would then take them back home to shell and start attaching to the hooks. Each line was about a mile long, and had hooks attached by means of shorter lines known as snoods. There were over 1,000 hooks per line and each fisherman had two lines. Children would pick fresh grass to line the baskets into which the lines were coiled, to prevent snagging on the wickerwork. In some fishing villages that had no quay, open boats would be anchored out in the bay. If the men had waded out, they would have spent a miserable day in soaking wet clothes, so their wives would carry them to the boats on their backs.

Longline fishing was used in deeper waters. The name was apt: lines could be up to 15 miles long and could carry as many as 5,000 hooks. Boats would set out for fishing grounds such as the Faroe Banks, north of Shetland, and would be at

⌃ A woman sits by her cottage door preparing shellfish for bait.

A Preparing for a fishing expedition involved the entire family, from the very oldest to the youngest.

◁ Fishermen preparing their gear for a voyage.

The line used for fishing was generally made from gut, but a variety of materials were used for the snoods, including cobbler's thread and horse hair, while some mackerel fishermen even went to the expense of using silk. The first innovation for paying out the line was the gurdy, a large reel turned by a handle, which presumably got its name from its similarity to the hurdy gurdy. Line fishing was distinguished by its versatility: it was as suitable for use with small rowing boats in coastal waters as it was for larger sailing vessels working far out to sea. Other forms of fishing usually required a more specialist boat and more elaborate, and, therefore, more expensive, equipment.

sea for weeks at a time, often in extreme conditions, surrounded by Arctic ice. The lines were baited at sea, with small fish such as young herring. Paying out the long lines was dangerous work as it was all too easy to be caught up by one of the viciously sharp hooks. Hauling the fish back in was physically demanding and as the fish came aboard they had to be taken off their individual hooks. In later years, strippers were used. The lines were pulled back through rollers, just wide enough to allow the hook through, but not the fish. In effect, the hooks were simply being ripped from the fishes' jaws.

▷ Women carrying their men to the boats.

THE SILVER DARLINGS

Silver darlings was the name given to herring, which, from medieval times, was the most important fish caught in British waters. The industry was mentioned in Domesday Book and it played an especially important part in supplying abbeys and churches. During the reign of William I, the Abbey at St Edmond claimed a tax of between 30,000 and 60,000 herring a year, and Edward I put in an order for 18,500 herring for his own household. The great English centres for the fleets were Lowestoft and Yarmouth, and in 1087 the Bishop of Norwich consecrated a chapel and paid for a minister specifically to pray for 'the fishermen who come to fish at Yarmouth in the herring season'. A year later it was granted a charter to hold a Free Fair for selling fish. The 1357 Statute of Herrings brought in the first regulations, which, among other rules, limited the

sale of fish to the hours between sunrise and sunset, and banned the sale of fish at sea. It specified that herring could only be sold in 'hundreds', defined as 120 fish – the fisherman's equivalent of the baker's dozen. It also provided the first mention of a smoked fish, the 'red herring'. It was said to be irresistible to rats, who would blithely follow the scent into a trap, hence it became synonymous with a misleading trail.

Herring fishing typically took place from small, open boats, but soon the North Sea trade became

> The women who followed the herring fleets often used what little spare time they had to knit.

Unloading herring from a steam drifter at Mallaig on the west coast of Scotland.

Women packing herring into barrels at Lerwick, Shetland.

dominated by a much larger craft, the Dutch 'buss'. This was a sturdy, round-hulled sailing vessel of up to 100 tons that could stay at sea for longer periods. This was thanks to the discovery in the 14th century of a means of preserving herring by a Dutchman, William Buckels. Buckels gutted and packed the fish between layers of salt – it was to revolutionise the fishing industry. The fish was no longer just a commodity to be sold in the area close to the ports, but could be packed into barrels and sent off to distant customers. In time it developed into an important export trade: herring from East Anglia would be sold in great numbers to overseas markets. The Russian merchants, important customers, had their own unique way of testing the fish. They would pull a raw herring out of the brine and take a bite from it.

The herring boats followed the fish down the east coast of Britain and by the end of the 18th century they were coming down from Scotland and round the coast from the south-west of England to join local boats. Catches were variable. In 1756, nearly 73 million herring were landed at Great Yarmouth, but in 1760 the catch was down to 7.5 million. The record catch of all times was in 1919, when an astonishing 45,345,800 fish were landed. But the dangers of overfishing were already apparent to some. As early as 1881, author J.W. de Caux warned that 'the sea is exhaustible'. His prophecy proved all too accurate, and herring stocks steadily diminished, almost to vanishing point, throughout the 20th century.

THE DRIFTERS

In 1809, the government decided to step in to help modernise the fishing industry. Up until then the British fleet had mainly consisted of small, open boats, often launched directly from a beach. The government now offered a bounty of £3 per ton to 'the owners of any whole-decked buss, or vessel, of not less than 60 tons burthen, being British built, owned in Great Britain … which shall be fitted out for, and actively employed in, the deep sea British white herring industry'. A further bounty was also paid on fish sold overseas. It marked the beginning of a vast expansion of the industry and a golden age for the herring drifter.

The drift net is very much what the name suggests: a large net suspended vertically in the water, attached to a boat drifting with the tide. The bottom of the net is attached to a cable, the warp that runs out from the side of the vessel sinking below the surface. The net itself is strung between vertical lines – strops – attached to buoys, so that the net itself is like a great curtain hanging in the water, with its top some 12 feet below the

⌃ The restored fifie *Swan*, built in 1910.

⌅ The two-masted drifter *Topaz*, a type of vessel known as a Zulu. Vessels such as this required a large crew to work them.

surface. A whole succession of nets could be attached to a warp and when the run was complete they would stretch out as far as a mile. The boat is allowed to drift, but kept on a set course by a sail on the mizzen mast, near the stern. The hardest part of drift net fishing is hauling in the nets with their loads of fish.

At the height of the fishing season, ports such as Yarmouth were so busy that it was said you could walk across the mouth of the River Yare from deck to deck: in 1918, 1,000 boats came down from Scotland to join 300 local vessels. One can imagine the scene as they all tried to get the best position, but avoid drifting into each other and entangling their nets.

Different areas had different types of vessel, but they all had one thing in common: they needed speed to grab a good place on the water in which to fish and, once the nets were in, get back to port as quickly as possible with the catch. It was

SUPERSTITIONS

Fishing has always been a dangerous occupation, so it is no surprise to find superstition rife among the communities. Certain words would never be spoken on board – 'rabbit', for example, was anathema everywhere from the north of Scotland to Portland Bill. 'Ministers' was another word not to use – you referred instead to 'the man in the black coat'. Meeting a dog on the way down to the boat was considered bad luck in some areas, and anyone who found a pigeon sitting on the boat was said to simply turn round and go back home. 'Whistling for a wind' was not just a saying, but something that was actually tried. If something unlucky happened while you were at sea, then the best antidote was to touch cold iron.

possible to catch too many fish, and sometimes the weight proved too much and there was little option other than to cut nets and leave them for a less fortunate boat nearby.

> The preserved steam drifter *Lydia Eva* heading out to sea from Great Yarmouth.

SETTING SAIL

Boats leaving the harbour at Great Yarmouth: the vessel in the foreground is raising its lugsail.

For centuries, the only way to move a fishing vessel was by oars or by sail. Open boats powered by oars were common. In Shetland, for example, the sixern is an obvious descendant of the Viking ship, which, as its name suggests, was worked with six oars and was perfectly capable of handling the conditions found out in the Atlantic. The most common types of sailing fishing boat were luggers and smacks. Staying in Scotland, one of the most popular herring drifters was the fifie. This is a two-masted vessel, with a dipping lugsail on the mainmast and a standing lugsail on the mizzen. The lugsail is the feature that gives this type of vessel the generic name 'lugger'.

The earliest sailing vessels had square sails hung from a yardarm set at right angles to the mast. The lugsail is attached to a yard suspended anything from a third to a quarter of its length, so that it hangs obliquely. In practice, this means that, when sailing, most of the sail is aft of the mast, which is efficient. The trouble is that when coming about if the sail was simply swung round, most of it would then be on the far side. So the yard is dropped, carried round the mast and raised again on the opposite side. This might seem ridiculously labour intensive, but there were always plenty of hands aboard a fifie because they were needed for handling the fishing tackle. A typical 19th-century fifie would have a crew of ten. This is a very efficient rig in terms of performance, and has the great advantage that it is easy to take down the sail and yard and clear them away, leaving plenty of space for the actual job of fishing. The standing lug is, as its name suggests, left in position during the drifting period.

The smack is gaff rigged: the mainsail is all arranged fore and aft behind the mast, the type of arrangement that you would see in a traditional dinghy. It is a rig with the obvious advantage that, when changing course, all that is necessary is to use the sheet, a line running from the bottom aft corner of the sail, to move the sail.

Sailing a fishing vessel required a high degree of skill and a good knowledge of the waters being fished. Boats fishing out of Yarmouth, for example, could be caught out if a strong wind from the north blew up. If they were unable to find shelter and were unable to round Winterton Ness they could be blown back onto the rocks at Cromer.

∧ Built over a century ago, the Cornish lugger *Barnabas* showing her paces.

∧ A fifie enjoying a good, strong breeze.

BARNABAS

Barnabas is a preserved Cornish lugger, built in 1881. In the 1980s the 100-year-old vessel was leaving Falmouth at the same time as a sleek, modern yacht when *Barnabas'* skipper recognised the man at the helm of the other boat: 'He was boasting about his boat in the pub last night. Let's show him what a proper boat can do.' Lines were tightened, the great mainsail filled with wind, and the old fishing vessel flew across the waves. The yacht, caught in the lee of the older boat, quite literally had the wind taken out of her sails and was left in her wake. It was the perfect demonstration of why such boats were prized and remained in use long after the invention of such 'modern' aids as the steam engine.

The men who went to sea were only a part of the story of any fishing fleet. There were many trades – boat builders, sail makers, merchants to name a few – all dependent on the fleet for their livelihood.

As the herring boats travelled to the fishing grounds they took with them a female army of workers. Their job was to gut and pack the herring as soon as they were landed, and as quickly as possible, to ensure the fish were kept fresh. It was recorded, difficult though it is to believe, that one Scottish herring girl could gut 60 fish a minute. Slicing away with extremely sharp knives was dangerous, and the only protection the girls had was to wind bandages round their fingers.

Great Yarmouth was one of the most important centres for herring fishing during a season that lasted through from September to Christmas. During this time, when the industry was at its height, up to 6,000 girls would come down from Scotland. Space was so tight that landladies housed them three to a bed. The girls were incredibly hard working, and were famous for the fact that when they weren't actually gutting and packing fish, they would be knitting, often selling the end products in local shops. They kept themselves to themselves, especially girls from the Isles who often spoke only Gaelic. At the end of the 19th century they were earning 10s a week, roughly equivalent to £50 a week today, out of which they paid about 3/6 for lodging. It was not

⋀   Women gutting herring.

much but they got a bonus at the end of the season depending on the numbers of barrels filled. Local shopkeepers also enjoyed an end-of-season bonus as the girls spent freely on gifts to take back home for Christmas.

The herring girls were only part of the workforce that depended on fishing. There were

YARMOUTH LIFE

O for Yarmouth bustle and hurry,
Time for nothing but making money,
But still it has its little joys,
Hippodrome, theatre, Gem and boys.

Elizabeth Bain, Scottish herring girl

◁ Scots workers taking a break in Great Yarmouth.

▷ Men mending their nets, an essential part of a fisherman's work.

always nets to be made and mended. Some places specialised in net making, notably Bridport in Dorset. Much of the work was passed out as a cottage industry, but some small factories also made nets. In a catalogue of 1884, Hounsell's of Bridport was offering nets in a variety of types and sizes, ranging from 10 fathoms long by 6 feet deep for £1 10s, to 50 fathoms by 12 feet for £11 5s. It is easy to see why fishermen protected their nets and mended them rather than buying new, when a big net cost the equivalent of some five months' work for a herring girl.

▷ An early 19th-century drawing by T.H. Williams, showing women sorting the catch on the beach near Teignmouth.

'HEVA! HEVA!'

'Heva! Heva!' was the traditional cry of the watcher on the cliffs, the huer, to tell the fishermen in the boats he had seen one of the great shoals of pilchards that would appear off the Cornish coast each summer. As an old rhyme put it:

> When the corn is in shock
> Then the fish are on the rock.

Pilchard fishing was a hugely important industry for Cornwall. According to a survey of 1827, it employed 3,272 fishermen and 6,350 shore workers. Luggers were the typical vessels of the region, often built with fine lines for speed. They were not, however, the only craft used to catch pilchard. The most effective method was by seine net fishing.

The enterprise began when the shoal was spotted, like some great stain on the sea, accompanied by squawking gulls and diving gannets. The huer gave his call and used signals to direct the seiners to the fish. This was a co-operative effort. At the head was the stop boat – a broad-beamed vessel slightly more than 30ft long crewed by six oarsmen and a cox – together with the main net, the stop seine – an immense affair, ¼ mile long and 33 yards in the centre. A second similar boat, the follower, came behind with a smaller net, the tuck seine, and all the equipment needed to secure the stop seine. A third boat, the lurker, was half the size of the other two and was the platform from which the master seiner conducted the whole operation. Once the shoal had been sighted, the aim was to enclose the whole mass of fish within the main

A good haul of pilchards, photographed c.1900.

Seine net fishermen relaxing on a Devon beach in the 1840s.

net, using the smaller net to close off any gaps. Once it was secured, the stop seine was towed to the shore, where it was hauled into shallow waters using capstans on the beach.

The great advantage of the system was that the entire catch did not have to be landed at once – part of the seine could be kept in the shallows with its haul of fish live, so that only enough fish was brought ashore each day as could be processed. There was also a useful bonus attached to pilchard fishing: hake are a predatory fish that were attracted to the tempting feast offered by the big shoals. The boats used long lines with baited hooks to secure this extra, very profitable catch.

Processing took place in the fish cellar, in which layers of salt were alternated with layers of fish, in a stack that could reach as high as 6 feet. After a month, the fish were removed and washed, then packed into barrels, with a large weight on top to drain away the oil. The barrels were regularly topped up with fish as the first batch was pressed down. The job of packing went to women known as 'fish maidens', who in the early 19th century were paid 1/6 (12.5p) to fill a barrel that might contain 2,500 fish. During the Napoleonic wars, when trade with Europe was cut off, the major export trade was developed with the West Indies, which at its peak amounted to around 200,000 barrels a year. In later years many of the fish were canned, as they still are today.

Seine nets being pulled in on the beach at Dawlish.

SHELLFISH

Fishing for shellfish has always been an important part of the fishing industry, usually carried out in small vessels that could be either sailed or rowed, and often launched directly off the beach. Different types of shellfish require different techniques.

Crab and lobster are trapped in pots, traditionally woven out of willow withies. There is a narrow entrance to the pot's larger chamber containing the bait, and once through the entryway the crustaceans are unable to get out. Fishermen would place a string of pots in suitable locations. The pots were weighted with stone to sink them to the seabed, and attached to a surface buoy with a small flag for identification. They were normally kept in place throughout the season, the fishermen coming out daily to collect the catch and replenish the bait. It was the latter occupation that often took up the majority of the worker's time, and not all fish were suitable: mackerel and herring, for example, were too soft to stay on the skewers that fastened bait inside the pots.

Various methods were used to catch fish for bait. In Start Bay, Devon, famous for its crabs, the most common method was using a form of seine known as a truck net. A 'hauling' boat, generally rowed by six men, set off from the shore with ropes and the net. Once the net had been taken out, often as far as a mile, it was shot, and teams of men hauled it back towards the shore collecting bottom-feeding fish such as plaice and dabs as it came. This was heavy work. A book of 1895 described the process:

> Here by degrees, the 2000 odd yards of line comes in hand over hand and is piled in great coils on the beach until suddenly the surface of the water breaks into bubbles and splashes like a great kettle boiling over, and then the seine appears enclosing a struggling mass of fish.

Fishing boats and lobster pots on the beach at Sidmouth, Devon.

An oyster dredger on the River Colne transferring its catch to a barge.

Oyster fishing is done by sailing smacks – small, gaff-rigged vessels, many of which have today already celebrated their hundredth birthday. The oldest oyster boat still afloat is *Boadicea*, an east coast smack built in 1808. Oysters were once far more plentiful than they are now, and were a valuable resource, protected by law. As far back as medieval times, there was a prohibition on fishing for them during the breeding season from April to July – hence the general rule about only eating oysters when there's an 'r' in the month. The boats would sail out to the oyster beds and use dredges, not unlike the harrows used on fields, to rake shellfish off the rocks. Today, oyster fishing in the Falmouth area is unique in that the boats can not use motors when dredging. South-east England, especially Colchester and Whitstable, has always been famous for its oysters.

The oyster beds on the Colne were so profitable that these two special police boats, *Prince of Wales* and *Alexandra*, guarded them.

SEABED DISPUTES

Oyster beds were often owned, just as farming land is. John Baxter, a Billingsgate fish merchant, owned oyster beds in the Teign estuary and managed them well, seeding the area with thousands of oysters for breeding purposes. In return, his lease of 1857 specified that only his employees had the right to take the oysters, and he was allowed to 'bring to justice all and every person' who was found trespassing on the beds or harming them. The local fishermen believed that no one could own land over which the tides flowed and tried to assert their ancient rights. The question came to trial in 1885, when 16 men and four women were fined £1 each. Other similar trials followed until the local fishermen had to accept the inevitable.

THE SAILING TRAWLER

There is no shortage of opinion on when trawling began in Britain: some claim that it was known in medieval times; others that it only became significant at the end of the 18th century. What most would agree on is that the modern age began with the introduction of the beam trawler at Brixham in Devon, a vessel that was to gain a reputation as one of the finest fishing vessels ever to work under sail.

Unlike drifters, which have a hanging curtain of net into which the fish swim, the trawlers dragged their nets along the sea floor, making them ideal for collecting valuable flatfish such as sole. In early days the trawl nets were quite small, but the Brixham trawlers were developed to work with beam trawls. The net, basically a large, open-ended bag, was attached to a wooden beam. It usually also contained pockets to trap the valuable sole, to prevent it simply swimming away. On the largest vessels the beams were up to 47 feet long, and to haul them across the sea floor required a powerful boat. That is what the Brixham trawlers were: vessels of 50 tons and more. The majority had a single tall mast, carrying mainsail, topsail and jibs attached to a long bowsprit, though the largest vessels were two-masted. With fine lines and a deep keel, these were vessels capable of handling all but the most severe conditions. On a recent trip a restored Brixham trawler returning to Britain from the Azores was caught in a fierce gale; one wave knocked the boat over so far that the tip of the mast hit a rising wave, but she came back up again – or no one would have been around to tell the tale.

△ A trawler entering the harbour at Lowestoft.

◁ One of four preserved Brixham trawlers being sailed by Trinity Sailing.

Brixham trawlers painted by the 19th-century marine artist Adolphus Knell. Although sail predominates, a small steam tug can be seen near the fully rigged ship.

Soon after they were developed, the trawlers began to move further and further from their home port, with colonies established as far away as Hull and the Irish coast. Their richest fishing grounds proved to be the Bristol Channel and along the Welsh coast, originally sending their catches back to Brixham for sale. In spring the vessels set off round Land's End and surviving records of the catches sent back from Padstow by train in 1902 give an indication of how profitable it was. In March that year, 12,700 pairs of sole were sent, in April 17,400 pairs and in May 8,300. This was good news for the crews, for they were paid by a share of the catch not by a regular wage.

Tradition has it that the Brixham trawlermen were the first to develop valuable new fishing grounds round the Dogger Bank, landing their catch mainly at Scarborough and occasionally Hull. It was decided that a new port was needed to cope with the increasingly valuable catches, and Grimsby in Lincolnshire was chosen as the site. A new railway line had been built in 1848, so fish could be sent by rail direct to the great fish market at Billingsgate in London. When the first new specialist fish dock opened in 1858 there was a score of vessels at Grimsby. By the end of the 19th century, there were over 800 sailing trawlers using the port, which was supplying a tenth of all the fish caught in Britain. But its success was very much based on the vessels first developed down in Devon.

THE STEAM AGE

Britain's very first steamboat puffed across the waters of Scotland's Dalswinton Lake in 1788, but the invention had virtually no impact on the fishing industry for a great many years. Far more important was the coming of the railways to the fishing ports. Now it was no longer necessary to rely on salting and pickling fish to send away to distant customers: fresh fish could be sent from the ports by rail. The early steamers were all driven by paddle wheels, mainly set on the sides of the vessel, which would have been inconvenient for fishing. Rather more significantly, it was difficult to adapt existing boats to take engines, so fishermen would have had to order brand-new vessels. Then when the steamboat arrived, they would have had to employ at least one extra crewman to look after the engine. On top of that were the running costs: coal was expensive; the wind was free. So it took almost 100 years from the first experiments with steam on the water before a paddle-steamer trawler came into use.

The steam engine did, however, bring a function that made life on the boats far easier. The steam capstan could be fitted to any vessel. It required only a small engine and was economical as it didn't have to be working all the time. It was invaluable for hauling in the heavy nets. An example can still be seen on the restored sailing fifie *Reaper* at the Scottish Fisheries Museum, Anstruther.

▼ A steam capstan being used to help unload the catch.

▲ The old and the new: A Scottish fifie passing a Yarmouth steam drifter.

By the 1880s, however, steam drifters and trawlers were being built, not with paddle wheels, but driven by the screw propeller, invented in 1838. This was ideal for fishing boats and the new steamers soon showed their worth. There were several obvious advantages to having a steam engine, the foremost being that when sailing craft were becalmed in harbour you could still puff off to fish. It also changed the way in which the fish were caught. A new method of trawling evolved using the otter net, in which the trawl net is held open by otter boards at either side of the net, instead of a beam stretching the full width. Because there was no need to stow away a cumbersome beam, far larger nets could be carried. The otter boards were kept up by water pressure, but if the boat speed dropped, they would sink down and the trawl net would collapse. A steamer can maintain a steady speed to counter this, which is difficult in a sailing boat subject to variable winds.

The steamers added two new members to the crew – an engineer and a stoker. As anyone who has ever tried it can testify, firing a boiler in the cramped engine room of a vessel pitching and rolling in heavy seas is no easy task. The basic rule of firing is 'little and often', to keep the steam pressure at just the right level. Let it get too high and the safety valves would blow, wasting the valuable steam; too low and the engine would labour. The engineer not only controlled the engine but was responsible for maintenance. At its simplest this meant oiling around all the moving parts on a regular basis. But he was also expected to carry out any necessary repairs during the many weeks when the vessel might be at sea.

By the start of the 20th century it was clear that the days of sail were coming to an end.

THE OLD FISHERMAN'S LAMENT

'Tis well an' fine for the steam trawler
To sweep the floor of the say,
But turble hard for the fisherman
As only sails the bay,
For the fish get scaircer and scaircer
An' hardly ait at all,
And what's to be catched with the
Seinin be hardly worth the haul.

Written in Cornish dialect in
1914 by Bernard Moore

LIFE ON BOARD

Life on a fishing boat depended very much on whether it was working inshore or away from the home port. Life on an inshore boat was simply about doing the work: going out in the morning, fishing and returning at night. It was very different on other vessels, where the crew might be living together in cramped quarters for weeks on end.

The skipper of a fishing boat is in a very special position. Jimmy Buchan in his autobiography, *Trawlerman*, recalled the advice he was given when he first took on his own boat: 'on the deck you work from your shoulders down; in the wheelhouse you work from the shoulders up.' It was his responsibility to get the vessel to the right place and shoot his nets at the right time to ensure a good catch. It took years to gain the experience to understand the movement of fish: sometimes swimming near the surface, at others near the seabed, depending on where they could feed most successfully. The crew depended on the skipper's skill to ensure a good catch so that they made a good living from their share of the sale. Inevitably, he was somewhat apart from the rest, and although he enjoyed the comparative luxury of having his own cabin, he could not share in the communal life of the forecastle.

Life for the crew was spartan, in the days of both sail and steam. In their quarters they slept on narrow bunks, ate their meals and, on the few occasions it was possible, relaxed. One very important person was the cook, working in the cramped galley. Meals needed to be hearty to provide the necessary energy for hard, physical labour. Fresh fish was an inevitable daily part of the diet, but there would always be meat for one

▲ A fine body of retired fishermen pose for the camera.

Fishermen casting their nets.

Unloading fish onto the quay.

meal as well. It was good, wholesome food, plain not fancy, though a writer who took a trip on a Scottish vessel in the 1920s had fried herring 'that any first class chef would have been proud of, and a light and tasty plumduff'. A vast urn of tea would be made in the morning with all the ingredients mixed together – by the end of the day it was an impenetrable black liquid with enough tanning to set the teeth on edge.

The work was unrelenting. The toughest job was hauling in the drift nets, pausing to shake out the fish, then heaving again, and repeating until miles of net were back on board. When not actually shooting or hauling in nets, there were always minor repairs to carry out and, on sailing boats, there was the constant job of trimming and setting sails.

For deep-sea fishing, the skipper had to acquire sound navigational skills. In the days before GPS and radar this involved a whole variety of different techniques. The magnetic compass showed the direction a vessel was pointing, which was not necessarily the same as the direction in which it was travelling due to tides and currents. Speed through the water was measured using a log, a triangular board thrown overboard attached to a knotted line. As the board floated, the line was paid out and the number of knots passing in a

given time gave the speed, hence ships' speeds are still measured in knots and entered in a logbook. The other guide to position was provided by the sun and the stars.

Once at sea, the fishing boat had to be a self-sufficient community. In the days before radio, there could be no communication with those back on the shore. No doctor could be called out to deal with an accident or illness, repairs had to be made at sea and the only other people you were likely to see were on the nearby boats fishing the same ground.

MEAT FOR THE VOYAGE

This was the order given to the butcher for a trip estimated to last 10–12 days:

2x5 lbs. roast beef; 2x5 lbs. stewing steak; 2x5 lbs. frying steak; 2x3 lbs. mince beef; 3x5 lbs. boiling beef; 3x5 lbs. sausages; 50 slices of sausage meat; 10 lbs. bacon.

From Linda Fitzpatrick, *The Real Price of Fish*, 2010

Fishing has always been a dangerous business. The stretch of coast between Land's End and Newlyn is much admired for its rugged beauty. But it is this rocky nature that has led it to be known as 'the fishing boats' graveyard'. Looking back through the records, Cornwall has a grim reputation. Between 1750 and 1950 some 250 vessels were lost along its coast. In March 1871, for example, the *Desire*, fishing out of Porthleven, was run down by a large ship, the *Corlic*, which sliced it cleanly in two. The teenage son of the *Desire*'s skipper was the only survivor. The great majority of the losses, however, came from vessels caught in storms and either driven onto the rocks or overwhelmed by the waves and sunk.

The most susceptible vessels to disasters at sea were the small, open boats used by many fishing communities up to the middle of the 19th century. On 18 August 1848, the weather on the Scottish east coast was fine and seemed perfect for fishing.

CAUGHT IN THE STORM

As Jimmy Buchan writes in *Trawlerman* (Sphere, 2011), he was once caught in a storm that threatened to sink even his modern trawler. As a great wave hit the vessel Buchan tried to keep control, but 'I couldn't hold on any longer, the force rippled through the wheelhouse, flinging me against the far wall, my back banging into the hard wood. A tide of charts, empty tea mugs and anything else that was loose rained down on me.' Deafened by the noise of the sea he thought the ship was going over, but she rolled back: they had survived. Looking back on the events, he wrote: 'When survivors talk about their life being in the balance, this is what they mean.'

⌃ The steam drifter *Strathalford* wrecked off North Head, Wick.

This was in the days long before weather forecasts were issued and there was no hint of what was to come when an estimated fleet of 800 vessels set out from ports all along the coast from Wick to Aberdeen. When the storm struck, those who could hurried to the nearest haven, but many were swamped while trying to enter harbour. Altogether, 124 boats were lost and 100 fishermen lost their lives.

The government appointed Captain John Washington of the Admiralty to conduct an

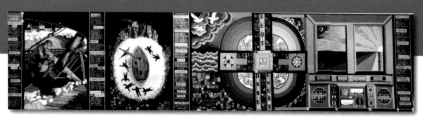

A tapestry commemorating the Eyemouth disaster of 1881.

A Lowestoft steam drifter crashing through heavy seas.

inquiry into why the storm had caused such damage. His report, published the following year, made two main recommendations. The first was that the government should offer a premium for the construction of bigger, decked vessels that would be less in danger of swamping by big waves. There was some reluctance on the part of the fishermen themselves to accept this idea: they were worried that big waves might just sweep them off the exposed deck. (It was not impossible, but one Devon fisherman was exceptionally fortunate. Although one wave washed him overboard, the next wave carried him back and dumped him on the deck.) The second recommendation was that the harbours should be improved to provide better protection.

The Scottish coast had been experiencing a spell of bad weather in the autumn of 1881, and so when Friday 14 October dawned with clear skies the fleets set out to sea from Eyemouth, even though barometers showed the pressure was falling. Around midday a violent storm hit. As boats turned and tried to run for safety, many capsized out at sea and others were thrown onto the rocks within sight of the crowds gathered on the harbour wall: 189 men lost their lives that day, 129 of them from Eyemouth itself. It remains Britain's worst fishing disaster.

The Fishermen's Mission is the only national charity that works solely with active and retired fishermen and their families. Offering services throughout the UK they help by providing financial, practical, pastoral and spiritual support, as well as being available day or night to respond to emergency calls to help fishermen in difficulties at sea.

The Fishermen's Mission is a registered charity No. 232822 and registered with the Office of the Scottish Charity Regulator No. SC039088

FISHERMEN'S MISSION

The founder of the Mission, Ebenezer Joseph Mather, was born in Stafford, about as far from the sea as one can get in England. But he and his family moved to London where he became involved with an evangelical movement helping seamen on the Thames. In 1881 he was invited by Samuel Hewett of the Short Blue Fleet to visit the North Sea fishermen. He was shocked by the deep distress in which many families had to live following accidents at sea, so he founded the National Mission to Deep Sea Fishermen. Today, the Mission continues Mather's work, providing practical help to fishing families.

LIFEBOATS

The lifeboat service has been closely tied to the fishing community since its inception, with generations of fishermen offering their services and manning boats for free. But the saving of lives began long before the first lifeboat was built. The fishermen of Deal and Walmer had a fine record of saving lives from ships wrecked on the Goodwin Sands, and rescues were carried out using the working boats of the region. Elsewhere it was not always altruistic, however: there was salvage money to collect and vauable cargos to be had, and some areas of the coast were famous for their wreckers deliberately luring ships to their doom.

In 1790 a Newcastle ship, the *Adventurer*, was wrecked in the mouth of the Tyne in sight of watchers on the shore. Sadly, the seas were too heavy for boats to go out to her; the ship broke up and the crew drowned. A local society offered a prize of 2 guineas to anyone who could design a boat 'capable of containing 24 Persons, and capable of going through a very shoal, heavy broken sea' in order to save lives. William Wouldhave, the parish clerk of South Shields, won the competition, but the committee were not entirely convinced and only gave him 1 guinea. They passed the job of putting the design into practise to a local boatbuilder, Henry Greathead.

△ Henry G. Blogg, the famous lifeboatman, who was awarded three RNLI gold medals and four silver medals for gallantry.

◁ The launching of the Buckie lifeboat in 1884.

The Buckie sailing lifeboat that saw service from 1922–49.

The first lifeboat, the *Original*, was launched in 1790. Greathead was to build 31 of these vessels, including the *Zetland* built in 1800 and now preserved in a museum at Redcar. She is a clinker-built boat, with a pronounced upward curve at bow and stern. Buoyancy chambers and cork fenders helped keep her afloat. She was powered by five pairs of oars and was kept mounted on a wheeled carriage so that she could be launched directly from the beach. She had a long working life, going to her last rescue in 1860.

The Royal National Lifeboat Institution was founded in the 1820s by Sir William Hillary. It co-ordinated all lifeboat activity around the coast and promoted the development of new designs that resulted in the first self-righting lifeboats. These are what we think of as the classic lifeboats with high-rising buoyancy compartments in bow and stern. They were mostly pulling-and-sailing lifeboats. That is, they could be both sailed and rowed; steam power was only introduced in the 1890s, to be followed by diesel engines.

One of the most remarkable rescue acts of all took place in January 1899, when a three-masted sailing ship, the *Forrest Hall*, was in trouble off the Somerset coast near Porlock Weir. A call went out to the nearest lifeboat station at Lynmouth, but the storm made it impossible to launch. The coxswain decided that the only hope of saving the 18 crew on board was to drag the lifeboat overland to Porlock to try and launch from there. This meant pulling the boat, which with its carriage weighed around 50 tons, for 13 miles. It had to be hauled to the top of Countisbury Hill, 1,000 feet above sea level, dragged over rough Exmoor tracks and then lowered back to sea level. A team of 100 men and 20 horses were needed and by the time they finally launched the boat almost 12 hours had passed since the first distress signal. The lifeboat crew then had to row for an hour through heavy seas to reach the *Forrest Hall*, but they succeeded and the crew were saved. It exemplified the spirit of the lifeboat service that no effort was too great if it meant lives could be saved. Sadly, sometimes it was the lifeboatmen themselves who never came back. As recently as 1981 the Penlee lifeboat was lost with all hands.

Fishing boats off Sidmouth in rough sea in 1830, by the celebrated artist J.M.W. Turner.

HOME FROM THE SEA

A fishing port can be anything from little more than a hamlet centred on a sheltered cove, to a large town with a well-protected harbour. Stone piers have provided shelter for centuries, some of which survive to this day. The Cobb at Lyme Regis was probably built in the 14th century, and a 16th-century map shows a structure virtually identical to the one we see today, though much of it has been repaired and rebuilt. Often no more than a single stone wall is needed to provide a refuge, however by the end of the 18th century, far grander harbours were being planned and constructed.

The famous engineer Thomas Telford was appointed to look at ways of improving the fishing industry of the Scottish Highlands. His most important project was the construction of a new harbour and the creation of a new town at Wick. A prominent feature was the brand-new kippering works, with built-in accommodation for the workforce. Work began in 1805 and soon Sir John Sinclair, the prime mover behind the scheme, was able to give an enthusiastic report on what had been achieved. 'Never,' he wrote, 'was money so well bestowed.' He reported that 1,500 boats were now working off that stretch of coast and 'above 100 decked vessels have been seen in the harbour at once, besides 20 or 30 at anchor in the bay'. Harbour improvements could, it seems, make a big difference.

▲ The little harbour of Portknockie, crowded with fishing boats.

Pulteney harbour, Wick, created in the early 19th century to boost the Scottish fishing industry.

A port, however, is much more than just its harbour: it is a community made up of the families of those who go to sea and others who support them. The larger ports might have their own fish markets, where the catch is sold, and many still do. At Newlyn, for example, fish is auctioned off at seven in the morning, so that it can be sent as fresh as possible to fishmongers around the country. In the days of wooden vessels, many ports had their own yards where vessels were built to suit individual owners.

The harbour at Crail, Fife, with its protective piers, is typical of small fishing villages around the British coast.

Building wooden sailing boats was an activity that changed very little over the years. Traditionally, the older boats were clinker-built, the strength of the hull depending on the overlapping planking. Later, carvel-built vessels became popular, where the main strength came from the frame that was then covered with planks that abutted each other to provide a smooth hull. The shipbuilders worked more by eye than by rule, selecting their own timber and marking it up to create the frames. Planks would be cut from trunks at a sawpit. The wood was laid across the pit, and a two-man saw was used: one man standing on top pulling it up, and the other down in the pit pulling it down, while sawdust rained down on his head. Shaping the curved frames was done with the adze, which was rather like a conventional axe in which the blade had been turned through 90 degrees. It was swung down onto the timber, cutting out curved fragments with every stroke. The builders worked in close co-operation with the fishermen: they knew them personally and had a clear understanding of just what was needed to make a sound boat. At the same time, they had to be ready to meet any specific requirements laid down by the new owner, no matter how quirky they might seem.

FISHING IN THE 20TH CENTURY

The first important change of this period came when a Swedish engineer, August Bolinder, designed the first successful diesel maritime engine. It was given its first British trial in a Thames lighter in 1910. All diesel engines generate enough heat during the compression stroke to create ignition, but they have to be started. The early engines were all of the hot bulb type, in which the fuel was vapourised by heating with a blowlamp. This must have seemed an alarmingly dangerous procedure, but the Bolinder salesmen had a spectacular safety demonstration. They poured a pool of oil onto the floor of the hold and threw in a lighted match: nothing happened.

The diesel engine was much cheaper to install and run than the steam engine, and existing boats could easily be adapted. In some areas, notably south-east England, steam engines were hardly ever seen: fishing went straight from sail to diesel. It brought new standards of efficiency to the industry, but in many areas the old steam drifters were still at work.

By the end of the 19th century, it was clear that fish stocks, especially herring, were in decline. During the First World War, deep-sea fishing all but came to an end. Fishing boats were called into service to act as minesweepers and were considered legitimate targets for German submarines and gunboats. Many fishermen enlisted in the Royal Navy reserves. The one good thing that came out of the pause was that it gave fishing stocks a chance to recover. For a time in the 1920s it seemed as if prosperity was returning, but soon the fish stocks began to dwindle again, and the Depression of the 1930s hit many fishing communities with particular ferocity. Families who had invested all their savings in their boats could no longer afford the cost of fuel, as catches were so low. Iron-hulled ships were sold for scrap and old wooden vessels dragged up onto the beach and broken up for firewood.

◁ The diesel trawler *Arctic Corsair*, built in 1960, survived being rammed by an Icelandic gunboat during the Cod Wars in 1970, and is now preserved in Hull.

A cheerful group of women, gutting and packing fish.

The Second World War once again saw many fishermen on war service, but when peace returned a new and different kind of war broke out – a Cod War. It began in 1951 when the Icelandic government, concerned about diminishing fish stocks, extended their territorial waters to 4 miles offshore. The British responded by banning Icelandic vessels from landing fish in Britain. Conservation, however, remained an issue and in 1958 Iceland increased its limit to 12 miles. Britain refused to accept the new limits and trawlers continued to fish in the disputed zone. The Royal Navy sent vessels out to protect the fleet, while Icelandic vessels did their best to harass the British trawlers.

In 1970 it appeared the matter had been settled when the Common Fisheries Policy was agreed in the European Community, but the dispute was far from over. In 1972 Iceland extended the limit to 50 miles, and British trawlers found themselves targeted by a new tactic, where Icelandic boats cut their nets so that they not only lost an entire catch but expensive gear as well. In 1975 the Icelandic limit was raised again, this time to 200 miles, and the following year the British government conceded the limit. In effect, deep-sea fishing in the Atlantic by British boats had come to an end.

The famous port of Grimsby had once seen hundreds of vessels working from its docks: in 2010 there were just 39 vessels registered, and 20 of those were under 10 metres long, working inshore. The glory days were over.

Modern inshore fishing boats at Walberswick, Suffolk.

PLACES TO VISIT

Alfred Corry Lifeboat Museum, Ferry Road, Southwold, Suffolk IP18 6NG

***Arctic Corsair* Rear of Streetlife Museum**, High Street, Hull HU1 1PS

Bridport Museum, The Coach House, Gundry Lane, Bridport, Dorset DT6 3RJ

Brighton Fishing Museum, 201 Kings Road, Arches, Brighton, East Sussex BN1 1NB

Brixham Heritage Museum, The Old Police Station, New Road, Brixham, Devon TQ5 8LZ

Buckie and District Fishing Heritage Centre, Cluny Place, Buckie, Banffshire AB56 1HB

Eastbourne Lifeboat Museum, Sovereign Harbour Marina, Pevensey Bay Road, Eastbourne, East Sussex BN23 6JH

Eyemouth Museum, Auld Kirk, Manse Road, Eyemouth, Borders TD14 5JE

Fleetwood Museum, Queens Terrace, Fleetwood, Lancashire FY7 6BT

Lossiemouth Fisheries and Community Museum, Pitgaveny Street, Lossiemouth, Moray IV31 6TW

Lowestoft Maritime Museum, Sparrow Nest Gardens, Lowestoft, Norfolk NR32 1XG

Lydia Eva* and *Mincarlo, South Quay, Great Yarmouth, Norfolk NR30 2RW

The Mo, Sheringham Museum, Lifeboat Plain, Sheringham, Norfolk NR26 8BG

National Fishing Heritage Centre, Alexandra Dock, Grimsby, Lincolnshire DN31 1UZ

Polperro Heritage Museum of Smuggling and Fishing, The Warren, Polperro, Cornwall PL13 2RB

Scottish Fisheries Museum, Ayles, Harbourside, Anstruther, Fife KY10 3AB

Shetland Museum, Hay's Dock, Lerwick, Shetland ZE1 0WP

Tenby Museum and Art Gallery, Castle Hill, Tenby, Pembrokeshire SA70 7BP

True's Yard Fishing Heritage Museum, North Street, King's Lynn, Norfolk PE30 1QW

Whitby Museum, Pier Road, Whitby, Yorkshire YO21 3RW

The Wick Heritage Centre, 18–27 Bank Row, Wick, Caithness KW1 5EY

Zetland Lifeboat Museum, 60 Esplanade, Redcar, Redcar & Cleveland TS10 3RW

The following organisations offer the opportunity to go to sea, either for day trips or longer voyages, on historic fishing vessels.

The Cornish Maritime Trust: lugger *Barnabas*; oyster dredger *Softwing*; and crabbers *Ellen* and *Sea Urchin*. www.cornishmaritimetrust.org

Lydia Eva, steam drifter www.lydiaeva.org.uk

Scottish Fisheries Museum: fifie *Reaper* www.scotfishmuseum.org

***Rosa and Ada*, oyster smack** www.rosaandada.com

Swan Trust: fifie *Swan* www.swantrust.com

Trinity Sailing: four sailing trawlers *Leader, Provident, Golden Vanity* and *Spirit of Britannia* www.trinitysailing.org